Little Book of
BIRDS

National Library of Australia

Canberra 1999

Published by the National Library of Australia
Canberra ACT 2600
Australia

© National Library of Australia 1999
Reprinted 1999

National Library of Australia Cataloguing-in-Publication entry

Little book of birds.

ISBN 0 642 10707 6.

1. Australian poetry. 2. Birds—Poetry. I. National Library of Australia.

A821.00803628

Edited by Julie Stokes
Designed by Kathy Jakupec
Printed by Goanna Print, Canberra

CONTENTS

The Bellbird Henry Kendall	Bell-birds	2
The Brolga John Shaw Neilson	Native Companions Dancing	4
The Cockatoo Judith Wright	Black Cockatoos	6
The Egret Judith Wright	Egrets	9
The Finch Thomas Shapcott	The Finches	11
The Friar Bird John Blight	The Friar Bird	13
The King Parrot Alan Gould	King Parrots	14
The Kookaburra Louisa Anne Meredith	Laughing Jackasses	16
The Lyrebird Judith Wright	Lyrebirds	18
The Magpie James McAuley	Magpie	21
The Pelican Mary Hannay Foott	Where the Pelican Builds	22
The Robin Douglas Stewart	A Robin	25
The Wagtail Judith Wright	The Wagtail	26
The Wren John Shaw Neilson	The Blue Wren in the Hop-bush	28
Acknowledgements		29

BELL-BIRDS

Henry Kendall (1839–1882)

By channels of coolness the echoes are calling,
And down the dim gorges I hear the creek falling:
It lives in the mountain where moss and the sedges
Touch with their beauty the banks and the ledges;
Through breaks of the cedar and sycamore bowers
Struggles the light that is love to the flowers;
And, softer than slumber, and sweeter than singing,
The notes of the bell-birds are running and ringing.

The silver-voiced bell-birds, the darlings of daytime,
They sing in September their songs of the May-time.
When shadows wax strong, and the thunder-bolts hurtle,
They hide with their fear in the leaves of the myrtle;
When rain and the sunbeams shine mingled together,
They start up like fairies that follow fair weather;
And straightway the hues of their feathers unfolden
Are the green and the purple, the blue and the golden.

...

Often I sit, looking back to a childhood,
Mixt with the sights and the sounds of the wildwood,
Longing for power and the sweetness to fashion
Lyrics with beats like the heart-beats of Passion —
Songs interwoven of lights and of laughters
Borrowed from bell-birds in far forest-rafters;
So I might keep in the city and alleys
The beauty and strength of the deep mountain valleys:
Charming to slumber the pain of my losses
With glimpses of creeks and a vision of mosses.

Extract reproduced from his **Leaves from Australian Forests**
(George Robertson, 1869)

THE BELLBIRD

Ebenezer Edward Gostelow (1867–1944)
The Bell Miner (Manorina melanophrys) 1930

NATIVE COMPANIONS DANCING

John Shaw Neilson (1872–1942)

On the blue plains in wintry days
  These stately birds move in the dance.
Keen eyes have they, and quaint old ways
On the blue plains in wintry days.
The Wind, their unseen Piper, plays,
  They strut, salute, retreat, advance;
On the blue plains, in wintry days,
  These stately birds move in the dance.

*Reproduced from **The Poems of Shaw Neilson***
(Angus & Robertson, 1965)

THE BROLGA

O. Stahl
Native Companion; Blue Wren 1909

BLACK COCKATOOS

Judith Wright (b.1915)

Each certain kind of weather or of light
has its own creatures. Somewhere else they wait
as though they but inhabited heat or cold,
twilight or dawn, and knew no other state.
Then at their time they come, timid or bold.

So when the long drought-winds, sandpaper-harsh,
were still, and the air changed, and the clouds came,
and other birds were quiet in prayer or fear,
these knew their hour. Before the first far flash
lit up, or the first thunder spoke its name,
in heavy flight they came, till I could hear
the wild black cockatoos, tossed on the crest
of their high trees, crying the world's unrest.

*Poem published in **Birds: Poems by Judith Wright***
(Angus & Robertson, 1962)

THE COCKATOO

William T. Cooper (b.1934)
Red-tailed Cockatoo 1970

THE EGRET

Ebenezer Edward Gostelow (1867–1944)
The Little Egret (Egretta garzetta); The Plumed Egret (Egretta intermedia) 1938

EGRETS

Judith Wright (b.1915)

Once as I travelled through a quiet evening,
I saw a pool, jet-black and mirror-still.
Beyond, the slender paperbarks stood crowding;
each on its own white image looked its fill,
and nothing moved but thirty egrets wading —
thirty egrets in a quiet evening.

Once in a lifetime, lovely past believing,
your lucky eyes may light on such a pool.
As though for many years I had been waiting,
I watched in silence, till my heart was full
of clear dark water, and white trees unmoving,
and, whiter yet, those thirty egrets wading.

*Poem published in **Birds: Poems by Judith Wright***
(Angus & Robertson, 1962)

THE FINCH

Sydney Parkinson (1745?–1771)
Loxia coccothraustes c.1767

THE FINCHES

Thomas Shapcott (b.1935)

A tiny spill of bird-things in a swirl
and crest and tide that splashed the garden's edge,
a chatterful of finches filled the hedge
and came upon us with a rush and curl
and scattering of wings. They were so small
I laughed to see them ludicrously gay
among the thorny stalks, and all that day
they teased me with their tiny-throated call.

They were a jest, a scampering of neat
brisk sweets, they were all such frivolities
I did not think to call them real, I was
too merry with their flight to see the heat
that angered their few days, to recognise
my own stern hungers in their fragile cries.

*Poem published in his **Selected Poems 1956–1988***
(University of Queensland Press, 1989)

THE FRIAR BIRD

Ferdinand Bauer (1760–1826)
Noisy Friar-bird (Philemon cornicualtus) c.1802

THE FRIAR BIRD

John Blight (1913–1995)

Bracken, sand and bush ... barely a dozen thoughts
Creation scattered here. Oh, who thinks like this?
How wizened is his mind! Thicker than these nuts'
rinds is his skull. He can't hear the hiss
of the mating snakes, where his danger lies
which, as his mind is blank, may too seal his eyes.

Here lives this world's mystic, knows its hidden smile
of the clean sands under unrevealing bush,
thigh-deep seas of bracken, sameness of each mile.
Who would heed the friar bird in the bottlebrush?
Who would ambush silence with such raucous clatter?
It is safer then for him to hear some other chatter.

But who can speak to lonely bush, who can speak with trees?
Only the friar bird may call, speak like this.
Blady-grass would cut the throats, put dead men at ease
when their tongues from talking grew black like his.
But the bush is listening still — it is worth while.
Here lives this world's mystic, knows its hidden smile.

*Reproduced from **John Blight: Selected Poems 1939–1990***
(University of Queensland Press, 1992)

KING PARROTS

Alan Gould (b.1949)

They've arrived.
That's all I am allowed to know.
Four, no six, they have materialised

trembling on the Mexican Hawthorn
as though the tree had just devised them,
six startling orchids,

or six jocund rascals, outrageous
in their green or crimson balaclavas
and crimson pantaloons,

tucking away their conifer wings,
eating with greedy disdain
like babies or comic strip bandidos.

My lawn is rubbished with half-eaten crimson berries.
Vandals. Solferino angels:
how can my eye stray while they remain

in creaturely candelabra
on a sky of nursery blue.
It's like a siege.

One cocks its head, as though to say,
'Don't worry. We are too brilliant to be real,'
then goes on eating from my tree.

They're gone. The branch skitters into stillness.
And I could spend a year behind this glass
longing for their return.

*Published in his **The Pausing of the Hours***
(Angus & Robertson, 1984)

THE KING PARROT

John Hunter (1737–1821)
King Parrot (Alisterus scapularis) c.1789

LAUGHING JACKASSES
(Gigantic Kingfisher)

Louisa Anne Meredith (1812–1895)

Three large grey birds sit up in a tree,
And they look as solemn as birds can be,
With very big beaks, and half-shut eyes —
Did you ever see anything look so wise?
Hark! all on a sudden one of the three
Bursts out a laughing! 'Ha, ha! Ho hee!'

Then another wakes up and opens his bill,
And his eyes are opening wider still,
He gives his feathers a shimmer and shake
Just to be sure that he's wide awake,
And then, as if some funny thing he saw,
Joins chorus, with 'Ho, ho, ho! Ha! haw!'

'Why are all three of them staring so?'
See — there's a black snake down below!
Gliding along thro' the dry brown grass —
But not very far will he safely pass;
Those solemn old birds are watching him go,
And chuckle for joy — 'Ha ha! Ho ho!'

Down they pounce! — they have got him fast! —
He writhes and twists, but that twist was his last!
He meant on some poor little bird to sup,
But the strong big birds have eaten him up,
And laugh, as they fly back again to the tree,
'Ha ha! Ho ho! Ha ha! Ho hee!'

Reproduced from **Grandmamma's Verse-Book for Young Australia** *(1878)*

THE KOOKABURRA

Sarah Stone (fl.1777–1802)
Great Brown Kingfisher 1790

LYREBIRDS

Judith Wright (b.1915)

Over the west side of this mountain,
that's lyrebird country.
I could go down there, they say, in the early morning,
and I'd see them, I'd hear them.

Ten years, and I have never gone.
I'll never go.
I'll never see the lyrebirds —
the few, the shy, the fabulous,
the dying poets.

I should see them, if I lay there in the dew:
first a single movement
like a waterdrop falling, then stillness,
then a brown head, brown eyes,
a splendid bird, bearing
like a crest the symbol of his art,
the high symmetrical shape of the perfect lyre.
I should hear that master practising his art.

No, I have never gone.
Some things ought to be left secret, alone;
some things — birds like walking fables —
ought to inhabit nowhere but the reverence of the heart.

*Poem published in **Birds: Poems by Judith Wright***
(Angus & Robertson, 1962)

THE LYREBIRD

Richard Browne (1776–1824)
The Mountain Pheasant 1819

THE MAGPIE

Lilian Medland (1880–1955)
Gymnorhina dorsalis; Gymnorhina leuconata c.1930

MAGPIE

James McAuley (1917–1976)

The magpie's mood is never surly;
Every morning, waking early,
He gargles music in his throat.
The liquid squabble of his note,

Its silver stridencies of sound,
The bright confusions and the round
Bell-cadences, are pealed
Over the frosty half-ploughed field.

Then swooping down self-confidently
From the fence-post or the tree,
He swaggers in pied feather coat
And slips the fat worms down his throat.

*Poem published in his **Collected Poems**
(Angus & Robertson, 1971)*

WHERE THE PELICAN BUILDS

Mary Hannay Foott (1846–1918)

The horses were ready, the rails were down,
   But the riders lingered still —
      One had a parting word to say,
   And one had his pipe to fill.
Then they mounted, one with a granted prayer,
   And one with a grief unguessed.
      'We are going,' they said, as they rode away —
   'Where the pelican builds her nest!'

They had told us of pastures wide and green,
   To be sought past the sunset's glow;
      Of rifts in the ranges by opal lit;
   And gold 'neath the river's flow.
And thirst and hunger were banished words
   When they spoke of that unknown West;
      No drought they dreaded, no flood they feared,
   Where the pelican builds her nest!

The creek at the ford was but fetlock deep
   When we watched them crossing there;
      The rains have replenished it thrice since then,
   And thrice has the rock lain bare.
But the waters of Hope have flowed and fled,
   And never from blue hill's breast
      Come back — by the sun and the sands devoured —
   Where the pelican builds her nest!

*Reproduced from **The High Road of Australian Verse***
(Oxford University Press, 1929)

THE PELICAN

Lionel Lindsay (1874–1961)
Pelicans 1938

THE ROBIN

John William Lewin (1770–1819)
Scarlet-breasted Robin (Petroica multicolor) 1800

A ROBIN

Douglas Stewart (1913–1985)

The vast cold silver sky
Gleams in the pool on the bluff
And the bush is grey after rain;
Little, oh, little enough

Is a morsel of wild bush robin
As long as your little finger
— A thing you could hide in your hand —
To feed the heart's great hunger

That could devour whole skies
Flaring with sunset red,
Mountains of fiery colour ...
Bright black eyes, black head,

And one white feather in his wing,
Flashing from twig to rock,
From rock to the shallow pool
That reels with the tiny shock,

The robin darts to bathe
Breast-deep in the sky's reflection,
And all that icy trance
Breaks in most sweet destruction.

Extract of poem first published in **Sun Orchids and Other Poems** *(Angus & Robertson, 1952)*

THE WAGTAIL

Judith Wright (b.1915)

So elegant he is and neat
from round black head to slim black feet!
He sways and flirts upon the fence,
his collar clean as innocence.

The city lady looks and cries
'Oh charming bird with dewdrop eyes,
how kind of you to sing that song!'
But what a pity — she is wrong.

'Sweet-pretty-creature' — yes, but who
is the one he sings it to?
 Not me — not you.

The furry moth, the gnat perhaps,
on which his scissor-beak snip-snaps.

*Poem published in **Birds: Poems by Judith Wright**
(Angus & Robertson, 1962)*

THE WAGTAIL

Ebenezer Edward Gostelow (1867–1944)
The Black and White Fantail (Willie Wagtail) (Rhipidura leucophyrs) 1931

THE BLUE WREN IN THE HOP-BUSH

John Shaw Neilson (1872–1942)

His home is in the wild hop, in brown and lemon green,
And all the orange followers of gold that come between:
He often says, to mock me, 'How slow of soul are you!'
And he puts into the broad sunshine his melody of blue.

The bushman's joke is gentle in long November days:
He fears the blue light of his friend may set the world ablaze;
And the blue friend says, to mock me, 'How slow of foot are you!'
And he puts into the broad sunshine his melody of blue.

All children who have seen him are gladder for all time:
He spells Romance and Comedy, his body is a chime;
And he often says to my heart, 'How thin of blood are you!'
And he puts into the broad sunshine his melody of blue.

*Reproduced from **The Poems of Shaw Neilson***
(Angus & Robertson, 1965)

THE WREN

Lilian Medland (1880–1955)
Malurus callainus (Splendid Fairy-Wren);
Malurus dulcis (Variegated Fairy-Wren) c.1930

ACKNOWLEDGEMENTS

The National Library of Australia wishes to thank the following for giving their permission to publish poems and pictures:

Alan Gould: his poem 'King Parrots'
HarperCollins Publishers: James McAuley's 'Magpie'; Douglas Stewart's 'A Robin'; and Judith Wright's 'Black Cockatoos', 'Egrets', 'Lyrebirds' and 'The Wagtail'
Rex Iredale: Lilian Medland's bird watercolours
Natural History Museum, London, and Alecto Historical Editions: Ferdinand Bauer's *Noisy Friar-bird*
Tom Shapcott: his poem 'The Finches'
University of Queensland Press: John Blight's 'The Friar Bird'

Front cover:
John William Lewin (1770–1819)
Spotted-sided Finch (Zonaeginthus guttatus) 1800

Back cover:
John Hunter (1737–1821)
Feathers of the Black Cockatoo's Tail c.1790